INCREDIBLE BASEBALL RECORDS

BY MATT SCHEFF

Published by The Child's World®
1980 Lookout Drive • Mankato, MN 56003-1705
800-599-READ • www.childsworld.com

Acknowledgments
The Child's World®: Mary Swensen, Publishing Director
Red Line Editorial: Editorial direction and production
The Design Lab: Design

Photographs ©: Shutterstock Images, cover, 1, 2, 23; Nick Wass/AP Images, 5; Mark
Duncan/AP Images, 6; Lenny Ignelzi/AP Images, 9; David J. Phillip/AP Images, 10;
Ted S. Warren/AP Images, 12; John Froschauer/AP Images, 15; Bettmann/Corbis, 16,
19; AP Images, 20

Design Elements: Shutterstock Images

ISBN 9781503808867
LCCN 2015958447

Printed in the United States of America
Mankato, MN
June, 2016
PA02307

TABLE OF CONTENTS

CHAPTER 1

Single-Game Records...4

CHAPTER 2

Individual Records...8

CHAPTER 3

Team Records...14

CHAPTER 4

Career Records...18

GLOSSARY...22

TO LEARN MORE...23

INDEX...24

ABOUT THE AUTHOR...24

SINGLE-GAME RECORDS

LONGEST GAME
8 hours, 6 minutes
Brewers at White Sox, May 8, 1984

Most games last nine innings. A few games need more innings to break a tie. It's very rare to get past 15 innings. In 1984, the Milwaukee Brewers and Chicago White Sox needed 25 innings to finish a game. That's almost three nine-inning games' worth of baseball.

The game was **suspended** after 17 innings. They finished it the next day. It took 8 hours, 6 minutes to play. But Harold Baines sent the Chicago fans home happy. His home run ended the longest game in Major League Baseball (MLB) history.

MOST RUNS BY ONE TEAM
30 Runs
Texas Rangers, August 22, 2007

The Baltimore Orioles led the Texas Rangers 3–0. Then everything changed. The Rangers scored five runs to take the lead. Two innings later, they scored nine more. They added 10 runs in the eighth inning. Then they scored six more in the ninth. That made the score 30–3. No team in **modern** baseball has ever scored more.

The long day for Baltimore wasn't even over. The teams had another game to play. Texas scored nine more runs in the second game of the doubleheader.

KENNY LOFTON

BIGGEST COMEBACK
12 Runs
Cleveland Indians, August 5, 2001

Seattle led Cleveland 14–2 in the seventh inning. It looked hopeless for the Indians. But they didn't give up. The Indians chipped away at the Mariners' lead. They trailed 14–9 entering the ninth inning. The Indians were down to their final out. But they kept hitting. They scored five runs to tie it. Then in the 11th inning, Jolbert Cabrera's single scored Kenny Lofton from second base. Cleveland had completed the comeback for a 15–14 victory.

The Indians' rally tied a record from early in MLB history. The Detroit Tigers came back from 12 runs down in 1911. The Philadelphia Athletics matched that mark in 1925.

MOST HOME RUNS BY ONE TEAM
10 Home Runs
Toronto Blue Jays, September 14, 1987

The ball was flying in Toronto as the Blue Jays beat up on the Baltimore Orioles. Ernie Whitt's second-inning home run started the fun. That blast was just the beginning. Six Blue Jays batters combined to hit a record 10 home runs in the game. Whitt led the way with three of them.

EMPTY SEATS

Imagine holding a game with no fans in the stands. It happened on April 29, 2015. The White Sox and Orioles played before a paid attendance of zero. Riots had occurred in Baltimore, and officials thought it was unsafe for fans to travel to the ballpark. So no fans were allowed to attend the game. That record could be tied, but it can never be broken.

CHAPTER 2

INDIVIDUAL RECORDS

MOST CONSECUTIVE NO-HITTERS

2 No-Hitters

Johnny Vander Meer, 1938

Few baseball fans knew who Johnny Vander Meer was. The Cincinnati Reds pitcher changed that on June 11, 1938. The 23-year-old lefty dazzled the Boston Bees for a **no-hitter**. Vander Meer was back on the mound four days later. He faced the Brooklyn Dodgers. And he did it again—back-to-back no-hitters. It had never been done before, and it hasn't been matched since.

MOST CONSECUTIVE SCORELESS INNINGS
59 Innings
Orel Hershiser, 1988

Los Angeles Dodgers pitcher Orel Hershiser had a season for the ages in 1988. Starting August 30, he didn't allow a single run in 59 innings! Hershiser led the Dodgers to the playoffs, where he added eight more scoreless innings against the Mets. But those innings don't count toward the official streak. He allowed a run in his first inning pitched in 1989. So the record stands at 59.

OREL HERSHISER

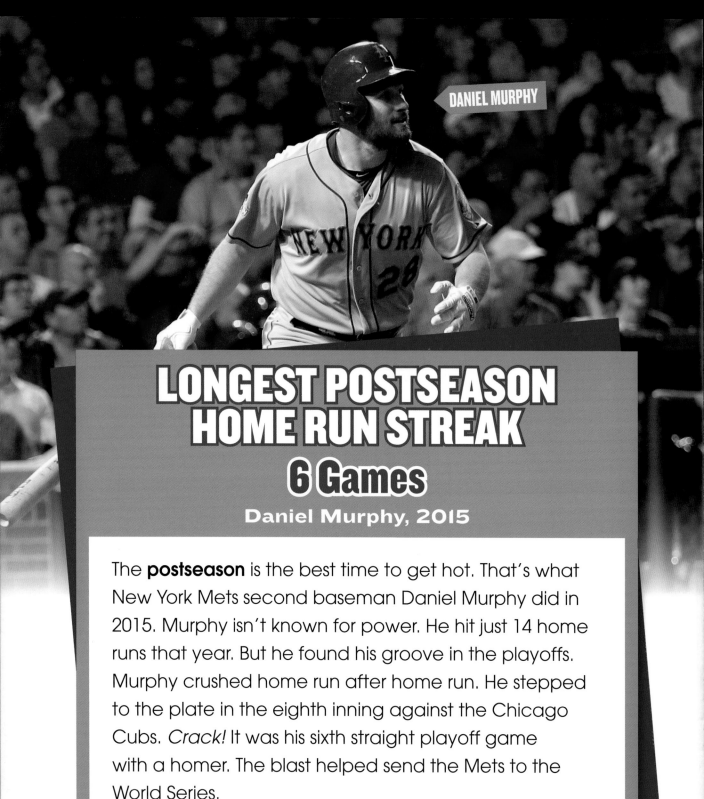

DANIEL MURPHY

LONGEST POSTSEASON HOME RUN STREAK
6 Games
Daniel Murphy, 2015

The **postseason** is the best time to get hot. That's what New York Mets second baseman Daniel Murphy did in 2015. Murphy isn't known for power. He hit just 14 home runs that year. But he found his groove in the playoffs. Murphy crushed home run after home run. He stepped to the plate in the eighth inning against the Chicago Cubs. *Crack!* It was his sixth straight playoff game with a homer. The blast helped send the Mets to the World Series.

LONGEST HITTING STREAK
56 Games
Joe DiMaggio, 1941

Joe DiMaggio was an all-time great. The New York Yankees center fielder was a 13-time All-Star. He led the Yankees to nine World Series titles. Yet DiMaggio was most famous for what he did over two months in the summer of 1941. DiMaggio thrilled fans by getting at least one hit in 56 straight games. No one has ever come close to breaking that record.

DiMaggio was used to long hitting streaks. He had a 61-game streak in semi-pro ball as a teenager.

EIGHT STRAIGHT

Three men share the regular-season record by hitting home runs in eight straight games. Dale Long did it first in 1956. Don Mattingly matched the feat in 1987. Then Ken Griffey Jr. did it in 1993.

ICHIRO SUZUKI

MOST HITS IN A SEASON
262 Hits
Ichiro Suzuki, 2004

Ichiro Suzuki was already one of the best hitters in Japan. He came to the United States in 2001 and quickly became one of the best MLB hitters, too. In 2004 the Seattle Mariners outfielder set the league on fire. He spent the season chasing George Sisler's record of 257 hits in a season.

Suzuki needed a huge finish to break the mark. He collected 26 hits over his last 13 games. Sisler's record was set in 1920. MLB teams played a 154-game season then. Suzuki played in all but one of the Mariners' 162 games in 2004.

MOST HOME RUNS IN A SEASON
73 Home Runs
Barry Bonds, 2001

The single-season home run record is one of baseball's most famous marks. Babe Ruth set the record with 60 in 1927. Roger Maris hit 61 in 1961. Mark McGwire shattered that record in 1998. He hit 70 homers. Three years later, Barry Bonds took the top spot. He crushed 73 home runs. Some fans think that the home run record means less than it used to. Many believe that McGwire, Bonds, and others used illegal drugs that helped make them stronger.

TWICE AS GRAND

Nothing beats a **grand slam**. One swing, four runs. It's a rare feat. Only 13 players have ever hit two in a single game. On April 23, 1999, Fernando Tatis of the St. Louis Cardinals did even better. He cranked out two in a single inning.

CHAPTER 3

TEAM RECORDS

MOST WORLD SERIES TITLES
27 Titles
New York Yankees

Young slugger Babe Ruth led the New York Yankees to their first World Series championship in 1923. Then the team known as the "Bronx Bombers" just kept winning. From 1949 to 1953 they won five titles in a row. In 2009, the Yankees won their 27th World Series title. No other team is close. Second place goes to the St. Louis Cardinals with 11.

MOST WINS IN A SEASON
116 Wins

Chicago Cubs, 1906, and Seattle Mariners, 2001

The 1906 Chicago Cubs were great. The team went 116–36. That's more than three wins for every loss. The 2001 Seattle Mariners matched that win total. Seattle went 116–46. Both were amazing seasons. Yet both ended in disappointment. The Cubs won the National League (NL) **pennant** but lost the World Series to the American League (AL) champion Chicago White Sox. The Mariners lost to the Yankees in the AL playoffs.

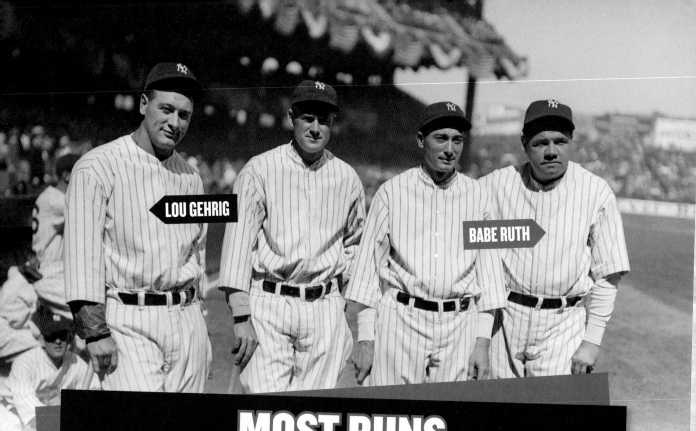

LOU GEHRIG

BABE RUTH

MOST RUNS
1,067 Runs
New York Yankees, 1931

The 1931 Yankees had a mighty offense. Babe Ruth and Lou Gehrig led the most productive lineup in history. They scored 1,067 runs in 154 games. That's almost 7 runs per game. Today teams play 162 games. Even so, no team has topped the Yankees' total.

But that high-powered offense didn't make much of a difference in the end. The Philadelphia Athletics won the AL pennant by 13 1/2 games.

LONGEST WINNING STREAK
26 Games
New York Giants, 1916

The New York Giants were a streaky team in 1916. They lost 13 of their first 15 games. Then they won 17 **consecutive** games in May. They capped their up-and-down season with a record-setting 26-game winning streak in September. The streak included one tie. Ties were relatively common at the time. But MLB doesn't count them as wins or losses. So the record stands at 26.

LONGEST LOSING STREAK

The 1961 Philadelphia Phillies had a rough month. They beat the San Francisco Giants on July 28. They didn't win another game until August 20. In between, they lost 23 straight games. No team since 1900 has lost more consecutive games.

CHAPTER 4

CAREER RECORDS

MOST CONSECUTIVE GAMES PLAYED
2,632 Games
Cal Ripken Jr.

Rookie third baseman Cal Ripken Jr. took the field for the Baltimore Orioles on May 30, 1982. It didn't seem like anything special. Yet it was the start of something big. Ripken played in every one of the Orioles' games for the next 16 years! In 1995, he played in his 2,131st in a row. That broke former New York Yankee great Lou Gehrig's record. Ripken's "iron man" streak ended on September 20, 1998, at 2,632 games. He finally got a well-deserved rest.

MOST CAREER STRIKEOUTS
5,714 Strikeouts
Nolan Ryan

Nolan Ryan was a true power pitcher. His blazing **fastball** often topped 100 miles per hour. In 1973, he struck out 383 batters. It's a modern-era record that still stands. Ryan pitched for 27 seasons. In 1990, he led the AL in **strikeouts** at age 43. Ryan finished his career with 5,714 strikeouts. Nobody else is close. Second-place Randy Johnson trails him by more than 800.

NOLAN RYAN

PETE ROSE

MOST CAREER HITS
4,256 Hits
Pete Rose

Pete Rose's nickname was Charlie Hustle. That's because he always gave his all. Rose joined the Cincinnati Reds in 1963. He started collecting hits right away. He kept hitting for 24 seasons. He led the NL in hits seven times. On September 11, 1985, Rose lined a single for career hit number 4,192. That broke a mark set by the legendary Ty Cobb. Rose went on to finish with 4,256 career hits.

MOST WORLD SERIES RINGS
10 Rings
Yogi Berra

Every player who plays for the winning World Series team gets a ring. A rare few get the chance to win more than one. But nobody has collected as many as catcher Yogi Berra. He helped lead the New York Yankees to 10 World Series championships. He earned a ring for every one of his fingers. That makes Berra baseball's greatest winner.

CY YOUNG'S UNBREAKABLE RECORD

What's baseball's most unbreakable record? Many think it's Cy Young's 511 career wins. From 1890 to 1911, Young won more games than any pitcher in history. Only one other pitcher has won 400. Pitchers in Young's time made a lot more starts than modern hurlers. So his record is almost certain to stand forever.

consecutive (kuhn-SEK-yuh-tiv): Consecutive things happen in a row without interruption. Orel Hershiser pitched 59 consecutive scoreless innings.

fastball (FAST-bawl): A fastball is a pitch that is thrown with little break and maximum speed. Nolan Ryan had a great fastball.

grand slam (GRAND SLAM): A grand slam is a home run with the bases loaded. Fernando Tatis hit a grand slam twice in one inning.

modern (MOD-urn): Modern things are related to the present time. Baseball's "modern era" began in 1900.

no-hitter (NO-HIT-ur): A no-hitter is a game in which the opposing team is held without a hit. Johnny Vander Meer threw a no-hitter in two consecutive starts.

pennant (PEN-uhnt): A pennant is a flag; in baseball it is symbolic of a league championship. The AL and NL pennant winners meet in the World Series.

postseason (POHST-see-zuhn): The postseason is a set of games played after the regular season ends. The MLB champion is determined in the postseason.

strikeouts (STRIKE-outs): Strikeouts happen when pitchers retire batters without them putting the ball in play. Nolan Ryan has the most career strikeouts.

suspended (suh-SPEN-did): If something is stopped for a short time it has been suspended. The Brewers and White Sox played a suspended game in 1984.

TO LEARN MORE

IN THE LIBRARY

Brown, Jordan D. *The Innings and Outs of Baseball.*
New York: Simon Spotlight, 2015.

Bryant, Howard. *Legends: The Best Players, Games, and Teams in Baseball.* New York: Philomel Books, 2015.

Rausch, David. *Major League Baseball.* Minneapolis, MN: Bellwether Media, 2015.

ON THE WEB

Visit our Web site for links about baseball: **childsworld.com/links**

Note to Parents, Teachers, and Librarians: We routinely verify our Web links to make sure they are safe and active sites. So encourage your readers to check them out!

INDEX

Baines, Harold, 4
Berra, Yogi, 21
Bonds, Barry, 13

Cabrera, Jolbert, 6
Cobb, Ty, 20

DiMaggio, Joe, 11

Gehrig, Lou, 16, 18
Griffey, Ken, Jr., 11

Hershiser, Orel, 9

Johnson, Randy, 19

Lofton, Kenny, 6
Long, Dale, 11

Maris, Roger, 13
Mattingly, Don, 11
McGwire, Mark, 13
Murphy, Daniel, 10

Ripken, Cal, Jr., 18
Rose, Pete, 20
Ruth, Babe, 13, 14, 16
Ryan, Nolan, 19

Sisler, George, 12
Suzuki, Ichiro, 12

Tatis, Fernando, 13

Vander Meer, Johnny, 8

Whitt, Ernie, 7

Young, Cy, 21

ABOUT THE AUTHOR

Matt Scheff is an author and artist living in Alaska. He enjoys mountain climbing, fishing, and curling up with his two Siberian huskies to watch sports.